ABOUT THE AUTHOR

Rhonda Sweat is an accomplished and experienced real estate expert who has been helping others navigate real estate for over 34 years. Rhonda started at a young age, she sold her first house at 16 years old and flipped her first house at 19 but she did not stop there, she has collaborated on hundreds of millions of dollars of real estate transactions in just about every niche', from owning a large real estate franchise to flipping to short-term and long-term rentals, as well as vacant land including multi-million-dollar development and multi-family properties. Rhonda's book *"Millionaire Mama: P.S. It's Not About the Money,"* is a back to the basics guide where Rhonda takes readers through an inspirational journey to show women how to build their empire through real estate investment, regardless of their age, income, or background. She prides herself as being an inspiration to all women by helping them change not only their lives but the lives of generations to come.

Rhonda is also the Founder of the **Millionaire Mama Club**, she prides herself on bringing women together to share, educate and inspire each other to build their empire through real estate investment.

The **Millionaire Mama Club** donates a portion of all proceeds to Domestic Violence Resources, as a survivor of domestic violence Rhonda understands the need to encourage and support women who find themselves caught in the domestic violence cycle.

Rhonda is passionate about inspiring women, but she is equally passionate about spending time on her family farm in Florida with her husband Chris and their son Chase, or just hanging out with family & friends in her favorite place, Boone, NC!

MILLIONAIRE MAMA

MILLIONAIRE MAMA

P.S. IT IS NOT ABOUT THE MONEY

RHONDA SWEAT

Book Design by Ruth L. Snyder

Edited by Ruth L. Snyder

Published by Rhonda Sweat Inc.

Hardcover ISBN: 979-8-9879713-0-7

Paperback ISBN: 979-8-9879713-1-4

Workbook ISBN: 979-8-9879713-2-1

E-book ISBN: 979-8-9879713-3-8

Audiobook ISBN: 979-8-9879713-4-5

CONTENTS

INTRODUCTION

Life moves whether you want it to or not. While circumstances beyond your control do happen, for the most part it is up to the person in the mirror (you) in what direction your life moves. You are the CEO of your life, and it is important that you realize this as early in life as possible. Life is kind of like a business. If you do not plan a path, you are not likely to live your life to the fullest. You need a well thought out plan to live your dream life. We have established that real estate is a lifestyle, so I will start with the vital details on how to get your life in order so you can become a Millionaire Mama! Millionaire Mama PS. It's Not About the Money is a book about life; it is a book about living your dream life!

"So many of our dreams at first seem impossible, then they seem improbable, and then, when we summon the will, they soon become inevitable."

-Christopher Reeves

People, in general, are always looking for something to make them whole or make them happy. Rarely do they "find it!" A lot of times they just wander aimlessly into whatever job or relationship that comes along. It is common that they do not even realize something is missing. They are just not happy in general, they just exist. They get by with the hand life dealt them. They do not even try to follow their dreams. They live their entire life not knowing the amazing feeling of true happiness or true love. That is no way to live your one and only life. The reason people do not find happiness is they expect to find it in a job, a spouse, their children and, in extreme cases, drugs or alcohol.

The problem is you will not find happiness anywhere except from within. Unfortunately, that is usually the last place people look. When a person does realize something is missing, rarely do they want to do the hard and often incredibly stressful work to find true happiness, because they must dig deep down inside. Quite frankly, it can be a painful experience. The other reason people do not find true happiness is they refuse to be held accountable for their own decisions. The truth is none of this is even our fault. It starts way before we even realize it. By the time we realize something is missing, we are already living the life we fell into. The cycle starts at birth and most people never realize it!

Ask yourself this serious question: Who do you love more than anyone else? This is a serious question that I want you to ponder. Your answer is probably, your children. But, see, you did not decide who to love first nor did you decide who to love the most. It just happens...and it started the day you were born. The day you were born, most often you loved your mom more than anyone else, then your father and then siblings, then your husband, after that your children. Rarely do people realize they do not even know themselves, much less love themselves. It was not until I was 50 years old that I realized I was not supposed to love them more than anyone else! I was supposed to love MYSELF more than anyone else! I spent so many years making everyone else happy. But in 2020, I realized if I had lived my entire life making myself happy by doing what I loved, and loving myself first, I could have made a much better impact and a much better life for those I love.

Just like we are born loving our mother more than anyone else, we are conditioned from birth to accept what is and not to reach for the stars, but that does not mean it is right. It does not mean it cannot change. It can change. You can change your path. You just have to want it badly enough to do the work to get to know yourself. You have to really get to know the person in the mirror (yourself) before you can reach for the stars and live the life you dream of.

"The future belongs to those who believe in the beauty of their dreams."

-Eleanor Roosevelt

The real estate lifestyle is a lifestyle many women dream about. It can be the best life there is for a working mom, because real estate gives you the freedom to control your own life. Two key factors in life are time and money; real estate allows you to control both.

This is more than an overview of how to get started in real estate. It is an overview of how to create financial security and long-term wealth to change not only your own life but for generations to come.

There are a ton of factors that decide the ultimate success in life, as well as real estate. We will go through the big ones here. There are so many intricate details. This is just the beginning, an overview of how to get your personal life in order for a powerful base, choose a niche, build a dream team, and start your REI business.

I was incredibly young when my mom switched from a nine-to-five to real estate, but I was old enough to realize the profound change it had on our life. I have a vivid memory of my mom coming home for lunch and, when she was ready to return to work, her car would not start and she started crying. As the sole provider of four children, she could not afford to lose her job, but she knew it was likely to happen if she could not get back to work on time. This memory is bittersweet and it makes me sad because those were extremely challenging times for my mom. At the same time, it makes me incredibly happy because it was not long after that day that our entire lives changed, 100% due to my mom's decision to go into real estate.

Real estate can change your life as well. If you want to learn how, grab a glass of wine and dive in.

DEDICATION

I dedicate this book to my mom and sister. They are the true heroes in society. Single moms doing their best every day to raise children who become productive adults is not an easy task.

My sister, Jamie Renee Perry, is my hero! She single handedly raised four children, as a single mom on a school bus driver's salary. She always had a side hustle to make sure they never wanted for anything, and they lived a good, stable life, with lots of love and discipline.

I wrote this book for moms like my sister who work hard raising their children but do not have a clue where to start when it comes to gaining true financial independence and building long-term wealth.

PREFACE

"Women don't have to choose between being present, and financial security!"

-Rhonda Sweat

Real estate has been my passion since I was fourteen years old. I sold my first house at sixteen, went to real estate school before I graduated high school and flipped my first house at nineteen. I have taught real estate for over twenty-five years.

My love for real estate started when my mom got licensed, but it took on a life of its own during my transition from middle school to high school. I met with a guidance counselor who told me I could get out of school two hours early everyday if I signed up for the On-the-

Job Training Program (OJT). At 14-years old, I knew I wanted FREEDOM & MONEY, and I wanted to be in control of both. If I got out of school 2 hours early, that would give me freedom, and getting a job would give me money! SIGN ME UP!!

I went to work with my mom in a real estate office back when there was no internet, fax machine, or cell phone. We carried huge books that were several inches thick full of the listings; and they were updated every week or two.

This was in the mid-eighties and things were quite different to what they are today. I recall how everyone dressed to the nines, their hair was perfect, their cars were high end and super shiny. I was fourteen and none of that appealed to me. The freedom appealed to me. I craved freedom.

Growing up in Tampa, Florida, I was from a middle-class family. They were mostly entrepreneurs who worked extremely hard for their middle-class lifestyle. Most of my friends, also middle class, had parents who punched a time clock. One of those parents worked at the same office from the time she was eighteen until she retired. She worked hard and climbed from the mail room to I believe vice-president. This was incredibly impressive. She lived an amazing life, had a second home, and traveled all over the world BUT she did not have freedom. She drove an hour to work and an hour home after working 8 hours, which is 10 hours a day, 5 days a week. That was a huge price to pay, in my opinion.

So, I realized early on that real estate provided money and freedom. I loved being a real estate agent and investor for this reason. I never missed my children's school functions; I volunteered my time on the PTA Board and the Soccer Booster Club. I was the parent who picked her children up every week at noon on early release. We went to the mall, the river or just to get ice cream but I was present! I had the freedom to be there whenever I wanted and definitely when I was needed. I made more money by being present than I ever would have as a 9 – 5 employee. It was a win-win.

"Real Estate is a Lifestyle, Not a Job."

-Rhonda Sweat

The number one thing I share with those who are interested in real estate is that "real estate is a lifestyle not a job."

You can literally make money in real estate by just living your everyday life. The best part is the better life you live, the more money you make. I am not a fan of the "free social media groups," but I do follow them, and I see so many women struggling to "find deals" or "figure out what to do with their kids." This blows my mind because the answer is easy for every single one of them, LIVE YOUR LIFE!

The key to being successful in real estate sales (or investment – but we will get to that) is to live the life you dream of and share your love for real estate with every person you meet and you will make money. Go shopping, go to the gym, volunteer at your children's school or the homeless shelter, attend church or a singles retreat, and share your love for real estate and you will do well. There is no complicated answer. It is actually remarkably simple, live the absolute best life possible, share your passion for real estate and you will make money in real estate sales or investment! There is no "secret formula."

There is, however, a lot to learn and a tremendous amount of hard work. But if you work hard, educate yourself and grow your network, all you need to do is live your life and you will connect with people who need your services and/or also love real estate.

Obviously, this plan works better when your life is organized and flowing well, but I have made amazing money in real estate even when my life was a total sh*t show, and you can too. My goal is to help you set your life up for success whether you are interested in sales and/or investment; most of the information is the same.

Remember, this is my story, and my opinions, but I am the first one to admit my way is not for everyone and there are other ways to do this—I am sharing my path. This is the path I have taught others and I have personally taken. It has proven to work well, so I wanted to share it with you.

Everyone's journey is different so take what serves you and ignore what does not. However, it is important to understand that what serves you today may not be the same once you are more knowledgeable and experienced. I have been in real estate sales and investment full-time for over thirty years, and I am still learning. There is always more to learn. Your perspective will change so make sure you glance back through to see if there are any nuggets of information that will help along the way.

PART I

BUILD A STRONG FOUNDATION

YOU FIRST! You cannot live your life your way until you get to know yourself. I have this discussion quite often, and most people think they know themselves. As mentioned, most people do not even realize that something is missing. But whether you think you know yourself or not, and whether you realize something is missing or not, diving deep inside and getting to really know yourself is the most important thing you can do to move forward towards the life you dream about. It does not matter if you grabbed this book because you know you need a life change, or because you just want to learn how to start in real estate. It all starts with YOU. The saying "stuff happens," has never been more accurate than now. Regardless of where you are in your life, regardless of how perfect or imperfect your life is, everyone has room for improvement. Get started, you can get to know yourself by asking these questions.

- What are my strengths?
- What are my weaknesses?
- What do I bring to the table?
- How well do I know myself?
- Who am I?
- Where am I?
- How did I get here?
- What do I want?
- How do I get it?

My hope is that whether you want to be an ultra-successful, multi-millionaire real estate investor or just want to add a few bucks to your budget, this information will help you move forward in Real Estate Investment (REI). Remember, it all starts with you and your mindset.

MINDSET MATTERS

*S*o many questions, a zillion different answers. My goal is to help you find answers to all these questions and many, many more...regardless of your age, education, income, or background. While I will guide you on the journey, ultimately your success is up to you.

If you set your mind to it, you can achieve it. Achieve what, you ask? ANYTHING YOU WANT!

-Rhonda Sweat

The key words are "SET YOUR MIND TO IT." Your mind is the most powerful part of the equation. Your mind can literally make you or break you. That is why you must keep your mindset in check at all times. When you really focus on mindset, you will find that sometimes the mind is a crazy thing. It will convince you to do or not to do something regardless of how much your heart and even your common sense tells you otherwise.

The worst part about mindset is it can be a vicious cycle and for most it never ends, especially those who live what I refer to as a generational disaster. When there are generations before you who have repeatedly done exactly what their heart or common sense told them not to do, it is easy to live to that standard. Not to mention, a lot of the traits found in the mind are hereditary. If you have negative hereditary traits, it is even more important to keep your mindset in check. I always say, for the most part, kids, employees, spouses, and people in general live up to expectations. If the bar has been set low, it is easy to live up to that expectation. For 50 years of my life I was stuck and, in many ways, I am still stuck. That is ironic right there, I am writing a book to help you, yet I admit that I am still stuck. The truth is, being stuck is a normal part of life. The big question is whether you will stay stuck or not.

Let us cut to the chase. Your mindset is the most important part of today, tomorrow, and everyday thereafter. Only you can keep it in check day after day, month after month, and year after year.

During the first FLIPHER Investment Summit, one of the attendees said something that stuck with me. She said,

"If you think you can, you will, if you think you can't, you are right!" This is a spin-off of this famous quote.

"Whether you think you can, or you think you can't— you're right."

-Harry Ford

Another attendee said, "I told my employee, "you will make a way, or you will make an excuse." It is up to you!" Today those words are truer than ever before because society has made it so easy to blame something or someone else. We blame others for everything. NOTHING is ever our fault. No one wants to take personal responsibility. Everyone makes excuses, when in fact it is all up to the person in the mirror - YOU. If it goes horribly wrong, it is your fault; and if it is absolutely amazing, it is your fault. Your future is up to you! Embrace it and make it everything you want it to be.

These pages are filled with my ideas of how to create a successful path forward in your life. You will not live the most successful version of you if you do not intentionally create your path forward. Hopefully, this book will help you create a direct path to being the most successful YOU possible and, if it is your goal, help you become the most successful real estate investor on earth. Your mindset will decide whether you make it or not. So ultimately, it is up to you to keep your mindset in check. How badly you want it and how hard you are willing to work towards it play into your success as well. Regardless of anything else, your mindset is the key factor and will continuously need work along the way.

Mindset, per definition, is the established set of attitudes held by someone. It surprises me that the dictionary uses the word "established" when it comes to mindset because in all reality your mindset is anything but established. It can change from the time you wake up, to the time you sit down on the porch to drink your morning coffee.

In general, I think the biggest factor in our mindset is poor habits. The worst part is a lot of them we were born and raised with, so we do not even recognize them as a problem.

It takes repetitive work every day. You are in control of your mindset, and you are the one responsible for changing it. The key is understanding that your mindset is a lot of different things. Sometimes we think something is wrong and then we realize it was not wrong; the way we were thinking about it was wrong. This is how mindset works, it is hard to keep track of and it changes often and without you even realizing it. It changes so often you do not even realize you have a poor mindset, which is why it is important to accept that mindset is daily work. It is important and constant work to keep your mindset in check.

FEAR was one of my biggest mindset problems when I was young. Due to childhood trauma, I never felt like I was enough. I constantly felt like I was letting someone down or I was not good enough. So, I learned when I was incredibly young not to fear anything. I learned the acronym FEAR is false evidence appearing real. I used it over and over when I was scared to do something, scared to make a move, scared to make a phone call, whatever the case may be I would literally tell myself this is false evidence appearing real.

- **False**
- **Evidence**
- **Appearing**
- **Real**

I would do whatever it took to push past it because everything I wanted was on the other side of fear. If I had not learned that little technique at an early age, I may have let fear consume me. You must try to avoid getting stuck or fearing anything. But when you do, and you will, only you can get yourself unstuck. You must stay in daily contact with yourself in order to control your mindset.

Confidence is a mindset, and it is the number one most important part of living a successful life but especially in real estate. You must be confident in yourself, and your ability to make decisions and most important your ability to pivot when you make the wrong decision. You cannot rely on anyone else to make your decisions for you! You must have the inner faith that you can do this and trust me you can!

2

PLAN YOUR PATH

*N*ow that you know how important mindset is, the next step is deciding exactly what you want to accomplish. What are your goals? It is incredibly important to determine what your goals are up front, or you will wander aimlessly. You cannot start your journey without a roadmap of where you are going.

Your goals are not written in stone, they can and will likely change. You will learn, you will gain experience, and your goals will change along the way. It is okay to change your goals, just make sure you always have goals.

Once you determine both your long and short-term goals, you can start creating the roadmap with the quickest path to success. It all goes back to the questions you answered in the beginning. This entire book revolves around those questions. If you have not taken the time to answer them, do so now. You cannot move on to where you want to be without answering those questions.

- What are my strengths?
- What are my weaknesses?
- What do I bring to the table?
- How well do I know myself?
- Who am I?
- Where am I?
- How did I get here?
- What do I want?
- How do I get it?

It is time to create your life intentionally, stop procrastinating, make decisions and TAKE ACTION.

Procrastination eats dreams;

do not allow it to eat yours!

-Rhonda Sweat

Your goals start with your WHY. Your WHY is the most important driving force from within. What drives you from within? There is no right or wrong answer. What means the most to you?

Financial security drives me, hence, PS. It's Not About the Money. For me, it is about the ability to pay for insurance, education, housing and making amazing memories.

Dream! Yes, I said dream—allow yourself to dream big dreams! Your dreams become your goals. This is your vision for your life. Do not think any dream is too big or too small, or that you cannot live up to it. You can do anything you set your mind to, and you should have your mind set to accomplishing your biggest and wildest dreams, because living the life of your dreams is oh so important. After all, you only get one life; and it is actually very short and goes by super-fast. If you do not create the life of your dreams, and live that life, you will live with regret.

I have a family member who has lived their entire life with horrific regret and guilt—so much regret that it has destroyed any chance she had at a happy, peaceful life. Regret is an ugly reality, when we do not live our lives the way we want. Do not fall into that trap.

You should have a vision of exactly what you want to accomplish. Your vision and your belief in yourself and what you can accomplish are powerful—the two fuel a fire like nothing else can. That fire will drive you, but you cannot allow the flame to dim or burn out. You must keep reminding yourself of your vision. It is your job to keep the flame burning.

Write your goals down into a business plan, and then into an actionable items list that you review often. Create a vision board and hang it where you can look at it daily. If you do not have your written goals and vision board in a place where you can look at them daily, then your mind will wander back to a familiar place. Unfortunately, that place is not always where our mind needs to be. It is a daily job to redirect your mind, or it will wander off and you will struggle to accomplish your goals.

3

YOU ARE NUMBER ONE

AVE YOURSELF FIRST!

Hopefully, you have flown on an airplane and seen the flight attendant's reminder to put your oxygen mask on first, before helping someone else with theirs. It seems reasonable, yet so many do not make themselves the priority. We live from one day to the next taking care of everyone else's needs but our own. You must stop worrying about everyone else first and make yourself the priority.

If you are not where you want to be, the first step is to accept where you are today, take responsibility and move on with a plan to get to exactly where you will be happy. This is the hard part; as mentioned before, a lot of the time we live our lives stuck in a situation that we know needs to change, but we do not take action to change it. We make excuses, we blame others, we do everything except take personal responsibility. Decide what you need to change and create a path forward. TODAY, take a stand.

"Stop singing the someone did me wrong song...

no one wants to hear it!"

-Rhonda Sweat

The first step is to "stop the bleeding," whether it is your bleeding heart, bank account, or anything else that is sucking the life out of you. STOP IT NOW and start taking personal responsibility RIGHT NOW. You are the CEO of your life. You are the only one responsible for yourself. You can try to blame someone else...anyone. But if your life is not going exactly how you want it to go, if you are not living the life of your dreams, talk to the decision maker right now. Look in the mirror and ask yourself (the decision maker) the following questions. Yes, the same questions because the answers lie within. And, when you get the answers, your entire life will change.

- What are my strengths?
- What are my weaknesses?
- What do I bring to the table?
- How well do I know myself?

- Who am I?
- Where am I?
- How did I get here?
- What do I want?
- How do I get it?

As the flight attendant reminds us, "You cannot save the world unless you save yourself first!" This was a hard lesson for me to learn, probably one of the most difficult. I was hell bent on saving my siblings, my friends, my children, my husbands. All I can think of is the Nicki Minaj song, "S" on my chest, 'cause I am ready to save him." I was going to save the world, but I never stopped to realize that if I were not okay, I could not save anything or anyone.

Who was going to save me? I will tell you who—NO ONE. It is funny how hindsight works; it really is 20/20. When I look back, I know if I had just made myself number one, put myself first, accomplished my own goals and made my own dreams come to fruition, I could have come far closer to saving everyone else. Notice I said far closer to saving them because, the truth is, I cannot save anyone and neither can you. We can help them save themselves, but they must want it and they must be willing to work for it and sacrifice for it.

That hindsight I speak of tells me that I should have allowed myself to take breaks, allowed myself time to recover, time to assess and address issues. But honestly, to this day, I still have not fully allowed myself to be weak. And, yes, it is okay to allow yourself to be weak.

In 2020 I was diagnosed with PTSD and it was no surprise. I had lived through trauma since the day I was born. I call it a generational disaster. One thing after the other, it never stopped, and I never stopped. I just kept rolling with it, going with it, pushing through it, fighting harder, even when I was fighting against things I could not control. Until the year 2020—that year was a life changer. In many ways, I think COVID-19 may have saved my life. I know that sounds ridiculous, but I was on fire, spiralling out of control, with no end in sight. When Governor DeSantis announced the COVID-19 quarantine, I decided to stay at my river house for 90 days. That decision is the best thing that ever happened to me. That time of reflection saved my life. Notice it was not by choice. I stayed at the river house because we were in quarantine. After quarantine, I stayed at the river house because I feared the unknowns of COVID-19. That pause gave me the time to reassess my life and really decide what was important to me and what was not. NOW, I realize, that is the number one thing that we need to do.

Everyone needs to consistently take breaks, pause to reassess their life, their goals, their direction. Ask yourself these questions; yes, you need to ask yourself the same questions over and over, forever.

- What are my strengths?
- What are my weaknesses?
- What do I bring to the table?
- How well do I know myself?
- Who am I?
- Where am I?
- How did I get here?
- What do I want?
- How do I get it?

When you answer these questions, remember do not think of your children, your husband, your parents, or your siblings. The question is what do you want out of YOUR life?

DECIDE WHAT YOUR DASH STANDS FOR

During the time in 2020 when I was reassessing my entire life, my friend lost a friend, and they posted on social media, "What does your dash stand for?" You know—the dash on your tombstone that represents the years you lived.

That is one of the things that really made me reflect on my future and my past. I started really digging deep into my soul for answers, asking myself tough questions. If I were to die today:

- What would people say about me at my funeral?
- How would my children feel?
- How would my husband feel?
- For what would my life have really stood?

The good news for me is, I am incredibly close to my husband and my children, so I know beyond any doubt that they know that my dash stood for loving them and my commitment to them. But we are so much more than wife and mother. We deserve more than that—we deserve to love ourselves; we deserve to make ourselves happy. Yet here we are day after day, month after month, year after year, worrying about what makes someone else happy. I have been through more traumas and more life crises than the average person, but I do not think that changes the thought process of putting yourself first. Think about it, especially those who have children. It is a natural instinct to put your children first, but really think about how much happier and content your children would be if you were genuinely happy and content. Take it from me. I am writing this book because I have literally lived this, seriously reflected, and studied it. I know beyond a shadow of a doubt that if you just stop and put yourself first, if you just push forward on your own goals, your own dreams and your own future, it will truly help the ones you love. The best path to help those you love is being the best version of yourself and living the life of your dreams. These questions will help you know where you are and what you need to work on:

- Do you feel guilty when you think about yourself?
- Do you feel selfish when you want time to yourself?

If you answer yes, STOP right now, and talk to the person in the mirror. Remind that person that everyone deserves to live their own life to the fullest. You deserve happiness and you deserve to live your life your way. You only have one life, and you deserve to live it any way you see fit. I have been in your shoes, and I am here to tell you it is crucial that you put yourself first. I do not care who you are, what you have done, nor what skeletons are in your closet. Do not be embarrassed; do not be ashamed. Be proud of who you are TODAY and what you personally want to accomplish. NOT as a mom, or a wife, or a daughter, friend, or sister, but as YOU. What do you want out of your life? Set those goals—set really, really big goals because when you have accomplished those goals.

and you are at the top, that is when you will genuinely be happy.

You will not genuinely be happy until

you are living your life, your way!

-Rhonda Sweat

Life is not a destination; it is a journey. Do not forget to stop along the way to just enjoy the moment, be proud of yourself, pamper yourself and reward yourself, and then move on to rock that next set of goals. This is how you live the life you dream about, the life you want. It is there, it is within reach, and you can get there, but no one can get it for you. You must get out of your own way and take control of your life, your future.

4

YOU ARE IN CONTROL OF YOU

*Y*ou are the boss of you. Regardless of where you are in your life, whether you have been through trauma or not, you are in charge of you and you are in charge of your future. Dreadful things happen to good people; accept it and move on. Accept that not everyone was meant to be your friend. Accept that some people are absolutely miserable in their own life and if you allow them, they will make you miserable as well. Do not allow it to affect you. I say your network is your net worth. Well, your self-esteem and your pride are as important as your network. Do not ever allow anyone to pull you down or make you feel less than you are or less worthy than you are.

"People come into your life for a reason, a season, or a lifetime."

-Brian A. "Drew" Chalker

Judgment is such an ugly part of life. I learned this late in life and it cost me dearly. DO NOT ever allow anyone to manipulate you or control your feelings. You are in control of you. If you allow someone to make you miserable that is not their fault, it is 100% your fault. I was so miserable for so long. My marriage was miserable, my friendships were miserable, and my business partnerships were miserable because I allowed other people to manipulate me and my future and even my children's future. It made me angry. It made me sad, and it diminished my self-worth. Do not allow it! If your dreams or goals do not align with your parents, your spouse or your friends, it is okay. Go talk to the decision maker (the person in the mirror) and decide how to proceed. Then move in a direction that makes you happy. Move in a direction that secures your future. I do not care if it is one day, or ten years, do not waste your life being miserable with or for anyone else, ever. You do not need anyone's approval or support to do what you want to do.

Have you ever heard the saying misery loves company? I think I have lived that more than anyone I have ever known. In reflection, I realize there were so many times in my life people I genuinely cared about just simply made me miserable because they were miserable. It had nothing to do with me. It was them. They were miserable, they were unhappy with their decisions, they were unhappy with the way they chose to live their life. I allowed that to affect my life. It was not their fault, it was mine. Key words: I allowed them to affect my life.

"Do not allow anyone to rent space in your head,

and if you do, make sure they are a good tenant."

-Author Unknown

I am not sure who initially wrote this quote, but it is on point. And, yes, I know this is hard. This is the hardest thing I have ever done in my life. I walked away from people that I would have died for, because I realized they were miserable and they were making me miserable. They did not care even after I tried talking with them. I tried over and over to explain my feelings. The bottom line is they did not care. I did not mean as much to them as I thought I did. When I first realized this, I was sad; actually, I was devastated and heartbroken but then I realized it was not their fault. It was my fault that I allowed them to disrespect me. It was my own fault that I did not walk away from them sooner. It was not their fault. You cannot blame others; you must take personal responsibility when you allow people to disrespect you.

Today, I no longer carry the same sadness for those who hurt me. It was my fault that I clearly cared for them and loved them more than they cared for or loved me. These problems come from our own expectations. Life is not fair, so do not expect it to be fair. Live your life, appreciate and be grateful for the good things and accept the bad or change it. Those are your only choices. It is your choice. Go talk to the decision maker (the person in the mirror.)

Whatever you do, never stay angry or bitter. This only hurts you. Anger, bitterness, and hatred will destroy you from the inside. There is nothing worth that. The Serenity Prayer reminds me to change what I can; accept what I can't!

"God Grant Me the Serenity to Accept the Things I cannot Change, the Courage to Change the Things I can, and the Wisdom to Know the Difference!"

-Reinhold Niebuhr

In reflection, what appeared to be the worst times of my life ended up being the best thing that ever happened to me. For example, when I decided to get a divorce, it was horrific. It was brutal but, in hindsight, it is literally the best thing that ever happened to me and my children. I moved on, I healed, and I used that experience to design the life I wanted to live. I do not live with regret. I do not beat myself up.

Just live intentionally and do your absolute best every single day. The rest will fall into place.

PART II

PERSONAL FINANCES

We started with YOU because without getting your mindset right, nothing else matters. I sincerely hope you dug deep inside to find the answers to the important questions. If you have done that deep inner work, you are on the right path to a successful future in real estate.

The first step to financial security and long-term wealth is to assess your finances. You should know your net worth at all times, in addition to your credit score and how much debt you have. Creating an overall financial analysis will help you later when we get to the REI section.

Hopefully you have a positive net worth. If you do not, you will need to decrease your expenses or increase your income, which you can do through real estate investment.

Now, I am not saying that you cannot get started before your personal finances are in order. I am saying it is easier if they are in order. And even if you get started, you will not be able to live the life that you dream of until you build a powerful base.

Personal finances are scary for a lot of people. When people are scared, they tend to ignore the monster that scares them. You know, kind of like do not poke the bear. Well, this bear has to be poked if you want to live a financially secure life.

It is unfortunate, but there are quite a few key life skills that are not taught in school or at home, and some of them are the most important skills that affect our future as adults. Young adults in America are making decisions at eighteen years old that can destroy their future for many, many years to come. It is a tragedy that in a lot of cases no one is guiding them, and they do not even have any idea how the decisions they make today will affect their entire life. Budgeting, taxes, credit, debt-to-income ratios are just a few of the important things that are not taught in schools or homes across America. The skills we are not taught are the very things that destroy our future before we even have a chance. These are two perfect examples. There are two main reasons a twenty-five-year-old cannot buy a house. The first reason, a car payment. Every single teenager should be taught how important it is to budget their money and how to save. They should know about debt-to-income ratios.

They should be told, "If you buy this shiny new car, it may prevent you from owning a house in the next 5 – 7 years."

-Rhonda Sweat

Granted, they may do it anyway, but at least they were told, at least they will not be sitting in a lender's office with a deer in the headlights look when the lender says your DTI (debt-to-income ratio) does not work. That means you will continue paying $1,400 a month in rent, instead of this $950 a month mortgage. That in itself is an oxymoron, but welcome to America.

The second reason a lot of people, not just twenty-five-year-olds, cannot buy a house is student loans. Whoever thought of this was one selfish individual. Who thought of the idea of putting these kids so far in debt that they may never be able to buy a house? My son is twenty. He gets inundated with emails and mail offering him student loans. The offer comes in big print that says low to no interest, or no payments for 2-years, and he can do anything he wants with the money. The student loan brochures have photos of students laughing and dancing. He can go on a cruise, buy a new snowboard, take his girlfriend to Vegas to ride donkeys up the mountain for her 21st birthday. (oh, never mind, wrong son.) The point is, this lack of knowledge is setting people up for failure before they even realize what is happening.

Let us take a step back. In order to live the life of our dreams, we need to learn about money: making money, spending money, organizing money. It is surprising to me that our high schools do not put more emphasis on teaching about money in general. In life, there is not a more important subject than money. Yes, you read that correctly. There is nothing in your life more important than money because money provides SECURITY. PS. It's Not About the Money, it is about the security money provides! Money provides a roof over your head, food in your stomach, a vehicle to get you back and forth to work, and life insurance, so if something happens to you, your children, spouse, parents, and fur babies are taken care of.

The saying is money is the root of all evil. I disagree with that. The lack of money is the root of all evil.

-Rhonda Sweat

Being broke is the root of all evil, but even worse than being broke is being greedy. There is a vast difference between being greedy and frugal or being greedy and smart with your money. Greed is when you want to take something from someone else; frugal is when you save your own money. One of the most important lessons you can learn in REI is in this paragraph. Be frugal, but do not get greedy. Greed does not look good on anyone. It takes a lot of people to power the wheels of real estate investment. Treat them well and pay them well. It will come back to you time and time again. In the end, you will make more money with this approach.

The area of personal finance includes a lot of vital details, and not one detail is more important than the other. So, get your copy of the Millionaire Mama Workbook so you can create your action list.

5

KEEPING UP WITH THE JONESES

a huge problem in society is we live beyond our means. We are constantly trying to keep up with the "Joneses" (our neighbors). This is a horrible way to live; do not do it. In a lot of cases, the Joneses are broke! Did you hear what I said? The neighbors with the flashy new Range Rover and Coach purse are probably broke; mortgaged to death and cash poor. Obviously, not everyone who owns a Range Rover or Coach purse is broke, but a lot of them are living paycheck to paycheck. They are not living a financially secure life.

When I was in high school, my mom owned a children's clothing store. I worked there sometimes, and I remember the most beautiful, well-dressed lady coming in to buy adorable clothes for her children. She drove a shiny new Jaguar, which did not have a huge effect on me, because my mom drove a shiny new BMW. What did have a huge effect on me was the paper food stamps falling out of her expensive, leather wallet. Her face was blood red, as if there were a huge white elephant sitting on her shoulder. She quickly gathered them without saying a word and rushed out of the store. I never saw her again. Food stamps are not the problem here. It is the Jaguar, and the nails, and the hair, and the brand-name clothes and purse. Those are the problems. I try not to judge—for all I know there could have been a reasonable answer, but from the look on her face it is very unlikely.

If you are serious about your future and about changing your financial position, you will start today under-standing that it does not matter how much money you currently make or have; and it definitely does not matter what anyone else makes or has. The only thing that matters is how badly you want to change your future.

- What is your financial situation?
- What can you afford?

Live within your means. Whatever it takes, live within your means. Drive the car that you can comfortably afford and live in the house that you can comfortably afford. Do not go buy what the bank says you can afford.

One of the things that drives me insane is how loans are underwritten. Underwriters ask you everything about your life. How much is your house or car payment, how much is your child support, how much is this and how much is that, but they never take into consideration your lifestyle. They never take into consideration that you may need to pay for a new roof in five years or what happens if you have a baby or a medical crisis.

It is your responsibility to underwrite your life. You are responsible for making sure that your financial position does not go to hell in a hand-basket because you choose to buy a new car or a new house. Just because an underwriter who has never met you says that you can afford it, does not mean that you can afford it. If you know in your heart that you like to travel, or have an expensive hobby, then when you decide to buy a house or a car, you need to take that into consideration. If you feel that you can only pay $1,800 a month for a mortgage payment, then do not agree to $2,200 a month because the underwriter says you can. Lives are destroyed when you are not in control of your own destiny or your own financial situation.

6

CREATE A BUDGET

*B*udgeting your money is a crucial step to financial security. In order to be free to live your future the way you want, it is important to assess your current financial situation. This means accounting for and planning for every dollar that you have, even when you do not have enough money to pay all of your expenses.

It is just as important to budget when your money is tight as when it is not. You will need to figure out your net monthly income and all of your expenses. All of them, including haircuts and morning stops at the coffee shop. You need to know every penny that you spend in a month. Once you have your income and expenses calculated you can use a piece of paper, an Excel spreadsheet or a fancy app to create your budget.

I must thank my former mother-in-law for instilling the importance of a budget in me at an incredibly young age. She and I never saw eye-to-eye on anything. However, I give credit where credit is due, and she taught me more about money than anyone else in my life. She taught me personal responsibility with money. She taught me that I needed a budget; and to carry a notebook with my budget in it, and that I should budget for today, tomorrow, a year, five-years, twenty-years, all the way to retirement. I admit none of this meant anything to me until I was thirty; but if she had never taught me this I would not be where I am today.

My former mother-in-law would loan my ex-husband and I money and make us pay it back with interest—not a lot of interest—just enough to make it officially a loan with interest. She required us to meet with her, show her our budget and show her that we had the means to pay it back before she would agree to the loan. It was an invaluable lesson that I appreciate to this day. Your budget is your road map—it guides you to long-term wealth and financial security. Regardless of how much money you make or if you make none at all, you should still have a budget and account for every penny of the money you spend.

My former mother-in-law was money smart. She taught me a lot of the money lessons that I still use to this day!

This is a big one; think of everything on an annual basis. When you add up how much you spend on an annual basis, it has more meaning than thinking on a smaller scale. Think about going to that coffee shop every day. The five dollars ($5) does not have much of an effect on that day but that one thousand-eight-hundred-dollars ($1,800) in a year is a significant amount.

COMPONENTS OF A BUDGET

Your budget consists of your income and expenses. This means all of it. I mentioned before you need a budget even if you don't have income. If you are spending money, you need to know where it is going.

The insignificant amounts add up. If you go to the famous coffee shop every day, that can add up to a significant amount of money, but people tend to leave it out of their budget, I mean it is only a coffee and a muffin. That coffee and muffin is $10.00 right now, that is $3,560 per year, and that is a lot of money to leave out of your budget!!

INCOME

You do not "need a job or income," to start your real estate journey. However, if you have a fantastic job that you love, you can continue to work while starting your real estate journey, but we will go over that in another chapter. Right now, we are talking about the income to pay your expenses each month.

You need to account for all of your income including child support, alimony, and side hustle income. My grandfather always told me if you watch the pennies, you do not need to worry about watching the dollars.

EXPENSES

When listing your expenses for your budget, always start with your needs: housing, utilities, childcare, and then add your wants. Do not leave this step out. It is unreasonable to think you will not spend discretionary money because you will. So go ahead and account for it up front, and do not cut yourself short. Lastly, you will add savings and debt repayment.

When calculating expenses, remember savings and emergency funds are not the same. You need each to include in your budget to reach optimal financial security.

Once you have compiled a list of all of your income and expenses, it is time to create the budget. It is best to create a monthly budget before the month starts. It is important to do a budget review each month and address any concerns. For the most part, your budget will stay the same; most expenses are the same every month. It is important to plan ahead and if you know you have a car repair or vacation coming up, put it in your budget ahead of time.

If you do not budget for these, they become last-minute crises and bad decisions that you cannot resist, like a trip to NYC with a friend, which are the things that kill financial security. Yes, I know NYC is a blast, but is it really worth allowing one weekend to affect your financial security? I think not. And the fact is, if you make really good decisions and get financially secure, you will be able to afford that trip to NYC anytime you want.

7

CREATING FINANCIAL SECURITY

inancial security is not as hard as a lot of people make it sound. It does take discipline and forethought. Basically, you cleared the first step when you set your goals, and the second step when you created a budget. Now you will simply take the steps to achieve your goals. They are not in any special order. They are all important. Work your way through them. Take your time to do it correctly. If you cannot get it correctly done all at one time, keep doing it a little at a time until you get it done.

CREDIT

It is important that you pay your bills on time because your credit is important. I know if you follow Dave

Ramsey, he says you do not need credit. He is wrong. You absolutely, positively need credit. You cannot buy a house, you cannot buy a car, or effectively start a business if you do not have credit. In fact, credit is reviewed to secure car insurance, life insurance, utilities, etc. Credit is reviewed to decide if you will need a deposit on your light bill or not. Credit is reviewed repeatedly. Credit is a huge factor in how fast you can scale your real estate investment journey. While the goal is to carry as little debt as possible, not all debt is bad. Debt that makes you money is good debt, so do not fall for the DEBT IS BAD routine. Start working on your credit score today.

The unfortunate situation in our country is the credit card companies drive your credit score, end of story! You can pay off five cars and two houses and it will not affect your credit score like a revolving credit card. So, you will need three credit cards. Start with one and work your way towards three even if you have to get a secured credit card. You will need to use credit cards to build your credit. The most crucial factor when building credit is to make sure you never and I mean never go over thirty percent (30%) of your limit. Going over thirty percent of your limit is the quickest way to destroy your credit score. If you have hospital bills or doctor bills, always make a payment plan. Do not allow them to go on your credit report. Once they are there, it will take seven years, and sometimes ten years for them to fall off. They will cause negative credit and that will affect your life in so many ways. Even if you pay them off, your credit score will still suffer because of those negative accounts.

Protect your credit. Do not allow it to get destroyed. If your credit is already destroyed, do not think paying off bad debt alone will build your credit back. The only way to build your credit score is to have available credit that you do not use. Credit card companies drive your credit score. Get the cards and never go over thirty percent.

BUY A HOUSE

Your monthly lease or mortgage payment should be no more than twenty-eight percent (28%) of your monthly income. Most often this is easier to reach when buying a home vs. renting. I hear a lot of real estate investors tell new investors not to buy a house. They say it frees up your credit and income to invest. I disagree! I highly recommend that you buy a house and preferably one that you can house hack and/or turn into a rental down the road. If possible, buy a duplex, a triplex, or a quad. This can be a part of your retirement later in life. It can be your safety net. But you need to buy a house. Moving is expensive and unless you own your house, there is a good chance that you will have to move every year or so. Property owners are constantly selling or raising the rent or something. Do not pay someone else's mortgage. When you pay rent, you are paying off someone else's house. The biggest reason to buy a house is appreciation; the longer you own it, the more it is worth. I do not care what the interest rate is, it is not 100%; when you rent you pay 100% interest. It truly blows my mind when I hear people say they are not going to buy because the interest rate is too high, really? Too high! Paying someone else's mortgage is too high. Do not do it. Even if it is not exactly what you want, even if it is not exactly where you want it, make your situation stable so that you can buy a house.

MORTGAGE

One of my biggest frustrations with the real estate mortgage industry in the United States of America is they only consider the payments on your credit report when calculating your debt-to-income ratio.

Two important factors that they do not consider is your lifestyle and home maintenance and repair. They do not calculate hobbies, travel, or dinner out several times a week. And they do not consider how you will pay for a new air conditioner if yours goes out.

It is your job to underwrite your life. You have a budget, you decide how much you can pay per month to own a house and you tell the mortgage broker that you will not go higher on a monthly payment. You have to determine your comfort level and do not allow anyone to convince you to change that. Remember we learned in an earlier chapter your budget is a key factor in your life.

INSURANCE

Make sure you are well insured but do not waste your money over-insuring. Make sure that you have health insurance because otherwise one medical situation could destroy everything. Make sure you have auto insurance. It is illegal not to and you do not need those problems. Also make sure you have life insurance so that if something happens to you and your children, your family will have a safety net to fall back on.

EDUCATION

It is incredibly important to budget for your education. I have offered a complete and very affordable mentorship where I was willing to help anyone change their entire future through real estate investment. It makes me sad to report how few people are willing to pay for that. Even worse is that some do pay for it and then they do not show up or take it seriously. Do not fall for, "Oh it is all free on the internet." Well, you know there is a ton of information about how to do brain surgery on the internet, but I do not think I will try that anytime soon and neither should you. Never stop educating yourself.

When I was a young girl, my grandfather told me, "Make sure you get educated because it is the only thing no one can ever take from you." When I think about where I am and where I have been, my drive to learn more is why you are reading my book. My drive to learn everything I could about real estate has taken me far, but I have had a coach or a mentor since the beginning. I am going to really show my age when I tell you I took the Carlton Sheets course when I was incredibly young—I want to say twenty. All the way back then I had the drive to do more. It is unfortunate but I will go ahead and admit here that not putting myself first is why I am not further in my journey than I am. It is not because I was not educated or I did not know. It is because of the other things that we have talked about in the course of this book—like marrying the wrong man or helping others who were not helping themselves.

Education is the key. Learn more about everything and anything you want to know. If you decide to go a different route, it's okay. You can still use that education. You literally never know where your path will take you. You never know who you will meet that will change your entire life. But, if you don't push forward, learn more, do more, then your path could stall. You could get stuck. And as mentioned in an earlier chapter, when you get stuck you must get yourself unstuck.

INCOME TAX

If there is anything to fear in this world, you should fear the IRS. The Internal Revenue Service is the last entity you want to hear from. The bad news is they are relentless on real estate investors. The good news is, if you have a hefty tax bill it is normally because you made a lot of money. PAY YOUR TAXES, but even more importantly, pay for tax planning. Later on in another chapter we will go through how and why you need a good accounting professional on your team, but it is important to at least mention it here while discussing expenses.

Whether you are a real estate agent or a real estate investor, you should make quarterly payments equal to more than you expect you will owe, because if you pay less, it will cost you dearly. Do not try to avoid paying taxes. Do not try to get creative. Just accept that if you make money, the IRS will get their share.

8

SHOULD I GET A REAL ESTATE LICENSE?

*T*his is one of the number one questions I am asked on a daily basis! I am including it here in the personal finances section instead of the REI section because this is an income question, not a real estate investment question.

I have been selling and investing in real estate since I was a teenager. Being a real estate sales agent has been the perfect career for me. There are very few people who can say, "I have had my dream job my entire life." It is a wonderful feeling. I have always controlled my time and my money, which is what I consider FREEDOM. A real estate sales agent is a great career, but you do not need to have a real estate license to be successful in real estate investment.

Would you hire a part-time agent to sell your most valuable asset? Hopefully, you answered no, and this is exactly why you should not get a real estate license if you do not plan to help others buy and sell real estate! -Rhonda Sweat

I have mentioned time and time again how perfect real estate sales has been for me over the past 30 years, but I want to make my opinion on this abundantly clear:

Do not get a real estate license unless you plan to make real estate sales your career. (In other words, you plan to help strangers buy and sell their homes.)

Real Estate Investors make far more money than real estate agents. So, if you do not plan to sell real estate as a career choice, then do not get licensed.

If you do decide to make real estate sales your career, do not get distracted by the money that you make in sales that you do not value investing in real estate. As I have said, Real Estate Investors make far more money than real estate agents, and they are far more financially secure. I wish I had taken real estate investment more seriously over the years, but I made so much money in real estate sales that I did not see my way to really taking real estate investing seriously until I was in my late thirties and gave up everything to get myself and my kid out of a horrific situation. I wasted a lot of time in sales when I should have been focused on investment.

I am not discouraging you from going into real estate sales if you need a career. As mentioned, the money is good but what is even better about being in sales is you are still in control of your time, and time is your hottest commodity. So, it is crucial that you spend your time the way you want to spend it. Do you want to clock into a 9:00 to 5:00 every day where someone else decides how much money you will make? Do you want to build someone else's dream company?

If the answer is no, then maybe real estate sales is for you. However, I do not want to make it sound like it is all "rainbows and butterflies." A real estate sales career is not for the faint of heart. It can be extremely hard. It can be time-consuming. It can be frustrating, but it can also be incredibly rewarding. It is a phenomenal way to live your life your way. If you have children, there is no better career. I have never missed a soccer game or a field trip. I mentioned this before, my children's events are actually where I found buyers and sellers. That's why I say real estate is a lifestyle, not a job. I volunteered in my son's school from kindergarten through 12th grade. I was always there, and I was always involved. To this day I think that is why we have a strong bond. I feel like my son knows how much he means to me because I have spent so much time with him.

Investors talk of getting licensed for real estate investment reasons. There is no reason to get licensed as a real estate investor.

PART III

REAL ESTATE INVESTMENT

MILLIONAIRE MAMA PS. It's Not About the Money is your guide to financial security and long-term wealth though real estate.

We have gone through the steps to getting your personal life in order because I believe you need a solid base to have a hugely successful real estate business. However, I do not think you should wait for your life to be to get started investing in real estate. You can start right here, right

now. If you work hard, be persistent and tenacious, you can build a successful real estate business while working on your personal life.

"You do not need money, credit, or anything else. All you need is an extraordinarily strong work ethic, which, by the way, is rare these days."

-Rhonda Sweat

There are a ton of factors that decide your ultimate success in real estate investment. Each and every decision you make will determine how fast you scale. This is just the beginning. There are so many intricate details. This book is just an overview guide. You will need to take each step and dissect it and build it to what fits your situation.

We go through how to get your mindset right, choose a niche, build a dream team aka network and start your REI business. It sounds complex, but it is actually quite simple. If you understand from day one that this is not a get rich-quick-scheme. Consistency and confidence are key to your success. You will need to plan, organize, make hard decisions, strengthen your network, then repeat every day and you will be successful in REI.

Everyone is looking for a get-rich-quick scheme or the easiest way out. I am here to tell you it does not exist. You will waste more time and energy by trying to get rich quick than by just working hard every single day to build your business.

You are reading this book which tells me that you are different from most people who honestly think that you can just Google everything and become wealthy. That is not how this works.

Google can absolutely destroy your life because Google lies. I said what I said. It is shocking at just how many people do not realize that anyone, anywhere can post any article that says anything on Google. So many people are in serious financial trouble by trying to Google their way through real estate investment. Other than the fact that Google lies, how do you Google something that you do not even know exists? Are you going to Google, how do I get rich in real estate investment? Okay, but how do you know all the intimate details that get you from point A to point B? Credibility is another key factor. The fact is you do not personally know the person who published the article. Social media has made it difficult to figure out who is actually an expert and who is simply amazing at graphic design. When you combine a great graphic designer with an article published to Google, it can be a recipe for disaster. The fact is every single person who publishes an article, a blog, or a book, etc. has their own agenda, experience, knowledge, and background. I even have an agenda. My agenda is different than most. I do have a proven history of helping others. My reputation precedes me. I have over 30 years' experience. I got my knowledge the good ole fashion way, I worked hard and studied hard.

"My agenda is to inspire women to gain financial security and long-term wealth in REI."

-Rhonda Sweat

While it is true that I would not be in real estate if it were not for my mom, it does not mean that I did not work extremely hard to gain the experience and knowledge that I bring to the table today. People assume I had an easy path because my mom was a real estate agent and my grandfather was a contractor. Nothing could be further from the truth. They did not give me anything. They did not serve anything on a silver platter, and there was no silver spoon. Just like most 19-year-olds, I knew everything so I did not listen to anything they had to say.

When I flipped my first house, I was like most teenagers and thought I knew more than most people. The truth is if I had listened to my family, I probably would have made more money on that house. The same goes for new real estate investors. If you listen and learn before diving in headfirst, you will scale faster and learn more. New investors are so anxious to get started that they make a ton of mistakes up front. These mistakes come back to haunt them down the road. My goal here is to share the steps a newer investor should take to help avoid those mistakes. I have said it multiple times throughout the book: Anyone, and I do mean anyone, who can read this book can invest in real estate, regardless of where you are right now.

The only thing that matters is mindset, but that does not mean there is not a lot to learn!

9

LEARN REI FIRST

I speak to new real estate investors every day. Typically, they have a pie-in-the-sky idea that all they must do is flip or buy a short-term rental and all of their financial problems are over. That is so incredibly far from reality. If you dive in headfirst before learning about leverage, reserves, funding, taxes, etc., your financial problems could get drastically worse, fast!

Real estate investment is one hundred percent about opportunities. There are always opportunities. There always have been and there always will be, so do not get caught up with the nonsense. Get away from the naysayers and the ones who say it is not a good market for investing in real estate. Run as fast as you can from people who are negative about real estate investing. I have never met a successful real estate investor who regretted investing.

Run as fast as you can from people who are negative about real estate investment.

-Rhonda Sweat

To take advantage of the opportunities, you need to learn how to be a real estate investor, a "real" real estate investor. This is the part that very few "GURUs" teach because a lot of them are not real estate investors; they are "teachers" or they did well at one niche and that is all they know. They have never been through a market shift, much less a crash, so what they are teaching may or may not matter in the long term. One thing that is for sure in life is CHANGE. The real estate market is cyclical, and it will shift. It is crucial that you learn all that you can, which is why we are here. You will learn the basics of becoming a successful real estate investor right here.

REI EDUCATION

When starting out in real estate investment, there is nothing more important than educating yourself. Education can be expensive but so can making costly mistakes. One of the mistakes that I see often is posting in groups looking for a free mentor. This is a horrible way to learn about real estate investment. You do not know what you do not know, so how do you know if the FREE mentor is teaching you the right way? How do you know that you want their FREE advice, guidance, etc.? Read that again.

DO NOT ASK FOR ANYTHING

WITHOUT OFFERING SOMETHING IN RETURN!

-Rhonda Sweat

Someone posted in a free group, "Is $8,500 too much to pay for a 6-month masterclass on commercial real estate?" My response, "There is not enough information to give an answer. There are some masterclasses worth $85,000 for 6-months and there are some that are not worth $85 for 6-months."

> **A mentor is someone who shares THEIR knowledge, skills and/or experience to help another to develop and grow.**

> **A coach is someone who provides guidance to YOU on your goals and helps YOU reach YOUR full potential.**

I highly recommend that you join your local real estate investors association to connect with someone who is successful in real estate investment, someone who has your vibe, to whom you can ask questions even if just in a group setting. But remember, a "mentor" answers your questions. It goes back to Google. How do you know what you do not know? How do you know what to ask? That is why you need a coach. A coach asks you questions and then gives you answers based on your goals. Once you are serious and you know you are ready to move forward and you know you want to continue the real estate investment path, you should hire a coach or join a coaching group.

I prefer group coaching over 1:1 coaching because it allows you to meet and network with others, and you learn from everyone else's struggles, solutions, and successes.

-Rhonda Sweat

Expect to pay for education. I have always followed the guideline that you should spend 10% of what you want to make every year on education. I want to make a quarter of a million dollars a year, so I spend $25,000+ on education every single year. Why would I do that after 30+ years of experience, knowledge and studying the real estate market full-time? Because you will never learn everything, no one will. It is the people who think they know it all who are the most dangerous and who will get in the most trouble. I learn new things all the time. This year, I learned a new investment strategy. I said no way in hell will that work. However, it is shaping up to be the most lucrative investment strategy of my entire career. Think about it, if Rhonda Sweat, a real estate investor and agent with over thirty years of full-time experience, learned an investment strategy that she had never heard of, imagine what you will learn when you put yourself in the right setting, around the right people. Never stop learning. Never stop paying for education, mentorship, and networking. Your knowledge and your network are two of the most sought-after forms of leverage.

10

THE MOST IMPORTANT WORD
IN REI

*L*everage, in my opinion, is one of the most important words you can learn because it takes a tremendous amount of leverage to build an empire through real estate investment.

Most investors only think of one definition of leverage:

"Use borrowed capital for (an investment)."

The definition I prefer is:

"Use (something) to maximum advantage."

The "something" that you can use to maximize your position in REI are the normal forms of leverage of credit and cash, but there is more to it than that. Every single real estate investment deal needs these forms of leverage: time, cash, credit, a deal or idea, network, experience, and education. Any one of these can maximize your position in real estate investment.

LEVERAGE

Time• The Deal • Cash on Hand • Available Credit • Good Credit Standing • Knowledge • Experience • Network

You have at least one item on the list, but you probably do not have all of them. It is extremely rare for someone to have all of them. In fact, I do not have all of them. I have very little extra time. I am always looking for someone who has time and wants to invest. Unfortunately, most people with only time as leverage are looking for immediate gratification. They just want to be paid for their time. They do not see the value in spending time now for payment at a later date. However, there are a select few who get it and those are my people, and they should be yours as well.

Like me, time is a commodity that a lot of people who have money or credit do not have. So, if you have time, you have great leverage. It is shocking how little value people put on their time. It is your hottest commodity. You can get money, credit, a deal over and over, but once you spend your time, you can never ever get it back. It is incredibly important to spend your time very wisely. Spend your time with the right people and sitting at the right tables. Just like when you spend time that you can never get back; when you get experience and knowledge, no one can ever take it from you. My granddaddy always told me, "Rhonda, make sure you get a good education, girl, because that is something no one can ever take from you!"

Now that you know how important leverage is and you know you need leverage, we will go through each of them. You need all of them to be successful, but I will start with your network. Your network is your most valuable leverage because with the right network, you can find everything else you need.

NETWORK = NET WORTH

Your network is your most valuable leverage. You know the saying, "It is not what you know, but who you know"? Well, that has never been more accurate than in real estate investment. You can be brand new, have no real estate investment knowledge or experience and still make a tremendous amount of money in real estate investment. You can be flat broke with poor credit and make a tremendous amount of money in real estate investment. An amazing network is not created overnight. It takes time and energy to meet people and connect with them for long-term gain, but this is the most important thing you can do when getting started in real estate investment.

I created the Millionaire Mama Club so I could surround myself with a network of women who share, educate, and inspire each other to build empires through real estate investment. I learned a long time ago that I can go further by working with others. PS. It's Not About the Money.

THE DEAL

Everything revolves around a deal, aka a transaction. Regardless of the niche you choose, you need a good deal to make money. This is one of the things a new investor with no other leverage can do. Teach yourself how to find deals. If you find a good deal, you can make money staying in the deal until the end or you can wholesale it. You will probably make less, but sometimes that is best depending on your situation. Sell today and make $5,000 or hold out for 6 months and make $25,000. Either way, you are making money in real estate.

CASH ON HAND

When I say you can invest in real estate with no money, we do not mean it literally. You definitely need money to invest in real estate, but you do not have to personally have money to invest in real estate. You can find someone who has cash to invest. There are several ways to do this. Find one person with enough money to fund an entire deal, find multiple people who can pool money for a deal, or find one person who has the money to get the deal done with a loan. This is one of the easiest things to find. There are a lot of people who have cash and see the value of investing but do not have the remaining pieces of leverage.

CREDIT AVAILABLE

Credit is not needed at all if you are dealing with an all-cash transaction. However, I would not try to do too many all-cash transactions. Available credit can be used to rehab a flip or furnish a short-term rental and, in some cases, buy a house.

CREDIT SCORE

A good credit score can take you a long way in real estate investment. It allows you to obtain mortgages, get vendor accounts for rehab or furnishings. It also allows you to get better insurance rates and sometimes skip the utility deposits. Investors are always looking to take on new investors if they have good credit

TIME

We have gone over this in depth, but time is a highly sought-after form of leverage. If you have time, you should have no problem moving forward in REI.

KNOWLEDGE

This book alone gives you knowledge which you did not have before reading it. The more knowledge you have on a subject, the better you will do in that subject. It is important to learn as much as you can. Knowledge is highly sought after in the REI world.

EXPERIENCE

When you have a good track record, it is easy to find real estate investors who want to collaborate with you. Your reputation will precede you when others see how well you do. This is why I do not cut corners on my projects. I want everyone to know I did it so they can count on it being done right. Experience is a form of leverage which cannot be bought, which makes it a highly sought-out form of leverage.

11

JOINT VENTURE,

NOT PARTNERSHIP

A joint venture is a contractual arrangement between two or more entities for a specific project. A partnership involves an agreement between two or more parties wherein they agree to share the profits as well as any loss incurred in a single venture. The best way to Move Forward in REI is by figuring out your strengths (leverage) and finding the people who have the strengths (leverage) which you do not have and form a joint venture.

Seriously, think about it. Why shouldn't we work together? Some investors have a negative view on joint ventures. Do not listen. Joint ventures are the number one way to financial security and long-term wealth. NOTICE I did not say partnering. There is no reason to "partner" in real estate investment. It restricts you and, in the end, can cause hard feelings. People change, life changes, change is inevitable. The thought that you and a friend will never change or grow in a different direction is unrealistic.

One of you will be more driven than the other. The driven investor finds advantageous opportunities that the other does not. The answer is to simply joint venture deal by deal. You can do twenty deals together, that is fine. Just do not think you will want to be with one person forever.

This is not a marriage; this is real estate investment,

and this is YOUR future.

-Rhonda Sweat

You will evolve as a real estate investor and you will gain more and more leverage, and eventually your goals will change. If you evolve and your partner does not, you will feel like you are letting your "partner" down. The answer is, do not partner.

In full disclosure, when I was young, I knew everything, like every other young person before me. It was not until I was in my thirties that I saw the value of joint ventures. After a horrific divorce where I gave up everything to get full residential custody of my son, I came back financially through joint ventures. I offered my knowledge and experience to those who wanted to learn to flip houses. It went extremely well. Granted, I brought a lot of leverage to the table. But you have leverage too. No, probably not as much as me and maybe not as much as the next person, but you have leverage.

Figure out what your leverage is from Chapter 10. All you need is one to get into real estate investment. Any one of these can make you a remarkably successful real estate investor. There are a ton of people out there with one or two forms of leverage, but they do not have the others. Once you figure out what your leverage is and you figure out what you need, find the person who has it and joint venture with them.

This is a notable example. I have coached a lot of traveling nurses. One of my traveling nurses had quite a bit of cash from a divorce settlement, but her credit really took a hit. Another traveling nurse had an excellent credit score, but no cash at all. I introduced the two, and they joined me in a joint venture. We had cash, credit, knowledge, experience, time, and a deal. It was a win-win-win.

12

ROI NOT DIY

his is the lesson new investors struggle with the most. FREEDOM is not freedom if you DIY!

One of my most used phrases is ROI, not DIY. ROI is your Return on Investment. DIY is Do-it-Yourself. If you go in with a DIY attitude, it will take you far longer to scale. Quite often, new investors confuse the two. They think if they do more of the work themselves that they are making more ROI, but that is not how this works. ROI is the profit earned from a real estate purchase after deducting the costs of the investment, which typically includes the purchase price and any additional expenses associated with repairs or remodeling. It does not mention "time spent doing repairs" for a reason.

CALCULATE ROI

**Net income divided by the total cost of the invest-
ment, or ROI = Net income / Cost of investment
x 100.**

The reason is because that has nothing to do with ROI. If
you paint the house yourself, then you should add up the
cost of material and your labor to enter in the expense
report. You do not claim that money as ROI. If you are the
agent who sells the house, the commission is not ROI; it
goes in as commission. You cannot mix ROI with DIY. ROI
is the remainder of what is left after all expenses are paid,
INCLUDING the money you made on DIY.

Freedom is the number one reason people start investing
in real estate. They want to cut free from their nine-to-
five jobs. They want the freedom to attend field trips with
their children or be there when they are sick, the freedom
to go on vacation more than once a year, the freedom to
have lunch with a friend, volunteer at a charity or to sleep
in when they are not feeling well or sleep in just because
you want to. Even though freedom is the number one
reason people want to invest in real estate, the first thing
every new investor thinks they want to do is flip houses.
Every new investor thinks DIY is the name of the game.

There is seriously little to no freedom in flipping. And the more DIY you do, the less freedom you have.

As mentioned earlier, I am often asked, "Should I get a real estate license to be a real estate investor?" This is one of the most common misconceptions new Real Estate Investors have. Unless you plan to sell real estate full-time as your job, in other words, you plan to market yourself as an agent and you plan to give up your evenings and weekends showing homes or listing homes, there is absolutely no reason to get a real estate license. As a real estate investor for the past 33 years, I would never hire a part-time realtor to sell my listings. Realtors can make you or break you. They are one of the most prominent members of your dream team, so why would you hire a part-time realtor, aka yourself, to sell your listings instead of a professional who has a system ready to go for maximum exposure?

If you decide to DIY, aka be your own contractor, your own painter, your own rehabber or your own agent, you are leaving money on the table and you are giving up freedom. HIRE PROFESSIONALS so you can get out and get on to your next deal. That is how you maximize your time and/or money. I am not saying if your husband owns a rehab company that he should not do the rehab. That is how I do so well at flipping houses. My husband owns a full-service rehab company. His shop looks like Lowe's, with every tool you could possibly need. He has experienced employees doing the work, which saves time and money.

My husband is very detail oriented; he and his crew brought my vision to life.

-Rhonda Sweat

It is important to realize the difference. I am a real estate investor; my husband is not. He owns a full-service rehab company, and it is expensive. The tools are expensive. The employees, the overhead, the insurance are all expensive. Therefore, unless this is something you plan to do full-time, do not do it. You are not saving yourself money because there is not one of those trades that make more money than a real estate investor. Not one. It is not worth it. Do not fall into that trap.

One of my favorite flips of all time is in the Atlanta area. I have never seen it in person, but I saw it in my 21k member REI group. I told the investor it was literally one of my favorite flips of all time. She did an amazing job. It was not until several months later when someone else asked her to post her numbers that I realized she had a zero ROI on this flip. She posted the numbers, and I was in shock. She made no ROI; it was negative ROI. Her husband was the general contractor, something he does for a living, and she was the realtor, which I think is something she does for a living. They took a while to make this beautiful home. They added a second story to an old single floor ranch house, and I am here to tell you they did an amazing job. However, when she posted her numbers, I pointed out she made no ROI; as mentioned, it was negative ROI. I had already raved about how much I loved the house, what a wonderful job she did. However, it was my job as a coach and host of the 21k 1st Time Investors Group to point out that she made a negative ROI. This investor had been coaching others. How could she coach others if she made a negative ROI?

Her husband made money for the rehab. She made money on the real estate sales commission, but there was absolutely no Return on Investment on that flip house. She may as well have spent all that time and far less energy working for someone else, as the rehab was going to cost the same. She would make the real estate commission regardless, so why spend all that time when there was absolutely no return on investment? She proceeded to argue with me, but the fact remains that she had no ROI on that deal. The worst part for me is she did not even know it. It is shocking to me that Real Estate Investors, some of them experienced, have absolutely no idea how to calculate ROI, because isn't that why we do this? I know personally I am not flipping a house if there is no return on investment. If we cannot find a flip, we will talk to others and work with them in a joint venture to be the contractor. But we will never flip a house where there is no return on investment.

13

CHOOSE A NICHE

e covered your goals in an earlier chapter because your goals will drive your niche. Go back and review your goals before you decide on a niche. Do not stray far from your initial decision, and never change your goals just to make more money. I named the book **Millionaire Mama PS. It's Not About the Money** because money is typically not what drives a person. When you read the earlier chapters, hopefully you have determined what drives you. Is it security, freedom, or something else? Regardless, it is typically not the money itself, so if you change the niche because you can make more money, you likely will be left unfulfilled and distraught. For example, if freedom is what drives you, do not choose flipping as a niche. It is the most time-restrictive investment niche. It does provide a nice cash flow, so you have to weigh which one is more important, and only you can do so.

PLEASE make sure you read the other chapters before choosing a niche. There are so many things to learn about real estate investment. Do not dive in headfirst until you understand exactly what you are getting into. Once you decide on one niche, do not jump around until you have that one mastered. Choosing one niche will be the hardest part of getting started.

When you are considering what niche you may like, the first thing to do is educate yourself about real estate investment in general. There is a ton of general information. Choose what feels good to you. Whether it is reading books, watching YouTube, joining a reoccurring mastermind, going to live REI trainings and meetings, etc., this will give you an inside look into what others are doing. It is important to start networking with other real estate investors during this beginning phase. Try to connect and network with those who are successful at the niche you are considering. Whatever you do, do not allow your pride to get in the way. Be humble and teachable! Each investor started as a new investor, and if you let your guard down you will be surprised at how many people will help you. There are a lot of people like me who really do care and want you to succeed. I have taken many people under my wing and got them started all by meeting them at a networking event and clicking with them.

It is important to realize their time is valuable, so do not expect them to mentor you and do not ask immediately. In fact, you should never ask anyone for anything until you have a connection with them and you know exactly what you need and exactly what you offer. Do not get offended if an investor does not want to mentor you. Most do not offer mentoring because it slows them down. It is hard to share every single detail with someone when your number one priority is just to clear the hurdles.

You will find your tribe, a group of people who you can connect with and grow with. It just takes time.

These are the most common choices for real estate investors.

WHOLESALE REAL ESTATE

In my opinion, every single person who wants to be a real estate investor should learn how to wholesale real estate first. I can hear your gasp, "But, Rhonda, I do not want to be a wholesaler". I did not say every single person should be a "wholesaler." I said, "Everyone who wants to invest in real estate should learn to wholesale." The word wholesale is greatly misunderstood. Today people think of wholesaling in a more negative light. It is common for people to think of wholesaling to mean someone uneducated found the property, slapped numbers on it, and now they are trying to market it to unsuspecting investors, but that's not what wholesaling means.

Wholesaling simply means you are buying something for less than market value to resale, or possibly keep in inventory. So, the first thing you should learn is how to buy real estate at wholesale prices, even if you do not have cash and even if you cannot get a hard money loan. Sounds like a total waste of time. It is not, it is one of the most lucrative and least time-consuming ways to get into real estate. Remember from the chapter on Leverage, a deal is a great form of leverage.

Typically, when you find a wholesale deal it is because you are providing a solution to a homeowner's personal situation. They need to sell the house and you need a deal, so it is a win-win.

Once you have the deal, it is up to you how you proceed. You can close on it or if the contract allows, you can assign it to another investor.

There is no reason not to wholesale. If you set yourself up as a successful investor you will find more deals than you can possibly buy.

Wholesaling can also be a business strategy. It can make you a lot of money. So, make sure you are set up as a business, so you can be prepared to take advantage of the tax write-offs.

But let me forewarn you, if you choose to wholesale as a niche, you really need a good accounting professional. There are very few tax write-offs, since most of it is done from the comfort of your home. That is a lot of taxable money. If you make $40,000 your first year, you could owe a significant amount of that to the IRS. It is so much easier to deal with what you owe if you are prepared up front. Regardless of which niche you choose, you should be set up as a business, even if it is a sole proprietor. It is best to be prepared with your dream team and everything is in place. Do not underestimate how fast you can make good money in real estate investment.

SHORT-TERM RENTALS (STR)

Short-term Rentals (STR) seem to be the latest craze. It is not as glamourous as it appears. Short-term rentals need to be understood from this perspective. When and if a market shifts, one of the first things that happens is people stop spending money on vacations and business trips. Even huge corporations often reduce their travel budget during times of uncertainty. It is particularly important to understand that you need another exit strategy. Do not go into short-term rentals thinking that it is a gold mine, because it is not. It is the quickest way to bankruptcy if you do not do it correctly. Short-term rentals appear to be a quick path to cash-flow, which could not be further from the truth.

If you are looking for a part-time job, that would be short-term rentals. If you have a lot of them, it could turn into a full-time job very quickly if you do not have automation and/or a co-host. I highly recommend a co-host if you are trying to scale the short-term rental game.

LONG-TERM RENTALS (LTR)

Back in the day, LTR were the most common real estate investment. You could buy a long-term rental, rent it out, pay it off with someone else's money and then have that to fall back on when you retire. Long-term rentals as an investment does work very well as a long-term strategy, so do not ignore it. It is a long game and that is what real estate is.

Regardless of what you choose as a niche, if you own an investment property, it should at the very least break even. If the short-term rental is not successful for any reason, you should be able to shift to a LTR to pay the bills. Long-term rentals could be the best choice if you have a full-time job that you enjoy and just want to get into real estate investment as a retirement.

FLIPPING

Flipping houses for profit is one of the most popular niches for new investors. They see experienced investors like me do it and it looks so easy. It is not easy. In addition to it not being easy, it is the most complex and time-consuming real estate investment niche. If you are looking for a full-time job, as mentioned, flipping is probably for you.

It is extremely important for you to watch the market when you start thinking about flipping. A market shift is not the time for a new investor to "figure it out." There are too many variables that can go wrong. It is also too hard to get back on the right path once it goes wrong. If you have your heart set on flipping, go to your network, find an experienced flipper and offer to joint venture. Remember to determine what your leverage is first. And never ask them to help you without offering something substantial in return. Experienced investors don't normally need new investor's leverage so make sure you are making it worth their while.

NOTES

The easiest way to describe a note is you become the mortgage holder. This is not a common niche for beginners, but it should be. This is one of my favorite ways for new investors to learn, and it is one of the safest as well. Notes are a fantastic way to make a great passive return on real estate. The upside is you will get paid on your money. And if you reinvest the profit, you gain compound interest, which is phenomenal? The downside to investing in notes is you do not own anything in the end. In my opinion, it is still the best choice as long as you can reinvest your profit/earnings. You can always mix these up, intertwine them and joint venture. If you decide to invest in notes, make sure you are the first lienholder and that you get the advice of your dream team, including your attorney and accounting professional.

14

REI IS A BUSINESS

*R*EAL ESTATE INVESTMENT is a business and should be formally structured as such. If you are a real estate investor you are an entrepreneur, and entrepreneurs wear many hats. It is important to have a business mindset from day one, even if you buy your first "investment property" as a second home in your personal name. If you set your business up early, it will help you scale later. Longevity in business counts. Start an LLC, open a business bank account, make it legal. You will reap the rewards later.

You absolutely must make sure you are following all the legal obligations of running a small business. There are a wide range of legal requirements for new businesses and startups, including financial regulations, tax obligations, and insurance requirements. It is your personal responsibility to make sure your company follows all of the legal responsibilities so you can get back to focusing on growing your business. Starting a business has a few key components. Listed here are the important components, but your state or municipality may have additional requirements. You will ask your local attorney and accounting professional about the local requirements. This is when you lean on your Dream Team. You will need "your" attorney and accounting professional to guide you through the process.

PLAN YOUR BUSINESS

Small businesses are still the backbone of society. And while that is becoming less of a fact by the day, it is important to know that the real estate investment business will never go away. People will always need housing. Nonetheless, it is important to consistently assess the future because economies change, needs change, real estate changes. And if you own a small "real estate" business, one change that you are not prepared for can change your future drastically.

SCORE

SCORE is a resource partner for the Small Business Administration. They offer a tremendous opportunity for new businesses, including help with your business plan, business structure and funding, which includes grants and small business loans. The appointment is FREE. I cannot stress enough, do not skip this step and do it in the beginning. SCORE WILL help you start your business and eventually get funding. It DOES NOT happen overnight. For example, if you started your business in 2019, you could have received $10k - $500k in "Covid" funding that, in some cases, was not required to be paid back, but a lot of real businesses could not get the funding because they were not formally structured as a business! DO NOT SKIP THIS STEP!

Create a business plan like you would for any other business. Seriously consider your vision, your mission, your goals, and incorporate that into your business plan. PS. It's Not About the Money. For me, my business has never been about the money. It was always about the security money brings. However, my mission and goals are most important to me. Being an amazing human being, especially a great wife and mother, are most important to me. I can say with extraordinary pride, I do not work for money; money itself does not drive me; I cannot be bought. I take great precautions to make sure that my husband and my children will be proud of my work, which is what matters most to me. So when a project comes up, if my heart is not in it, if it does not make me feel good inside, I will not do it. This is the very reason we start with mindset and YOUR WHY, and this is the very reason I say, "Always ask yourself, is my WHY bigger than my WHY NOT!" Your "WHY" is most important, so never lose sight of that.

Entrepreneurship is not the easiest path, but it can be rewarding not only financially, but it can bring extraordinary pride and peace to your life. When I transitioned to helping women gain financial independence and long-term wealth, it was not easy transitioning from 100% real estate sales and investment. My income took a serious hit, but I was driven by my own sister's story. I felt I had to do something to help women get out of places where they feel stuck, with no hope for the future. In 2021, I conducted two-hundred and eleven - 1:1 interviews with women across the country. Hearing their stories and listening to their desperate pleas for help pushed me to continue the path, and today I can say I have no regrets.

So, regardless of how hard it gets, stick it out, stay on your path, fight harder, and it will evolve into exactly what it is supposed to be.

PICK A NAME & MAKE IT LEGAL

Naming a business may seem trivial, but it is one of the most important decisions you will make. A great business name should reflect your business' identity. It is costly to change your business name, and any goodwill you have will be gone. So get it right from the beginning. First impressions, good or bad, last forever. There are no do-overs. Your name is important, and it should reflect who you are and what you do. Your goal should be to evoke emotion.

What do you want to share with the world? Create your name around that. Do not make it too specific in case you expand, and do not make it too broad so that people understand what you do. Catchy names or acronyms work well. My company was Sweat Equity Group, obviously a play on my last name and the well-known real estate industry standard of sweat equity. I also played with starting a company named FRED, which stood for Florida Real Estate & Development. Both were catchy names, which worked well in the industry. Millionaire Mama is a name I created in 2020. Millionaire stands for "security" in a lot of people's minds, and Mama because that is what my son calls me. Ultimately, I decided on Rhonda Sweat, Inc. because I have a wide variety of opportunities, and it was hard to produce a name that reflected all of them, so I went with branding my name.

Regardless of what name you choose, make it legal. Start a legal business. And once you are ready to reach for the moon, trademark it. Trademark is an unbelievably wild world. It is not easy to understand and, unfortunately, attorneys do not always know all the answers or follow through. It is a long and tedious process.

BUSINESS CREDIT

It is important to build a business. It is equally important to obtain business credit. While it is not necessary, it is easier to get commercial funding than it is to get residential funding. Also, if you keep using your personal credit, your score will eventually take a dive and then it will be almost impossible to get business credit.

Business credit takes a while to build. So, your business start early and start building the credit. You may need to be a personal guarantor in the beginning. It will not take long for the business to have credit of its own. I personally know someone who has $200,000 of business credit. He can buy a house with cash. This is an incredibly powerful position in REI.

CLOSING

I hope the information in this book helps you Move Forward in REI! Investing in real estate is scary but it is the best thing that you can do for yourself and your future, as well as the future of those you love. So, get started as a soon as possible. Even if you take baby steps and then do a little more and a little more until you have accomplished your goals. The Millionaire Mama Workbook will help you take action by taking you through the book and guiding you step-by-step.

Remember this is just my opinion on how to Move Forward in REI. Take what works for you in your life.

FINAL THOUGHTS

*L*ife in general throws so much at us every day. It is hard to stay focused because there is more content than ever, but most of it is meaningless. Life is what you make it and everything you do in life has pros and cons. There is nothing in life that is all rainbows and butterflies. The good news is you can live your life your way, and it all starts back at Chapter 1 with Mindset. You will want to revisit that Chapter because your Mindset is the only thing that can stop you from living out your wildest dreams. If you remember this, you will be fine. Stuck is a Mindset Problem. If you get stuck, do the mindset work to get yourself unstuck. There is no way to avoid getting stuck because mindset is incredibly powerful and, as mentioned before, it constantly needs work. Whatever you do, do not use "stuck" as an excuse not to be held accountable. It all goes back to the quote, "If you think you can, you will. If you think you can't, you are right." It is all in your mind. You must stay in constant contact with yourself. Talk to the decision maker daily, give that person in the mirror a pep talk every single day! Remind her that she is beautiful, she is smart, she is a warrior!

Seriously, talk to yourself, and listen to the answers.

- Self, are you doing well?
- Self, are you happy?
- Self, why aren't you accomplishing your goals?
- Self, why are you doing this or that?
- Are you into working out?
- Meditation yoga?
- Reading?

It is important to be well balanced. One of my favorite books is *The 5 Love Languages* by Gary Chapman. If you have not read it, it is a must read. It will tell you so much about why humans get "stuck." We get stuck because our "love language tank is low." If you do not even know you have a love language tank, how do you fill it? I have worked on this consistently for 30 years even with my children and my husband when they are stuck, or they are frustrated or something is not going the way they want in their life. We reflect on the situation, and it is quickly discovered that one area of life is not on point, it is not up to par, It is not going according to plan. Once you get that area back on track, you will be unstuck. The problem comes when we are not aware of what is not going according to plan. It can destroy you. Your mindset is the only thing that can truly destroy, so go back and read Chapter 1. If you do so, you will live the life of your dreams.

My last piece of advice is stay focused on your WHY. As long as your WHY is bigger than your WHY NOT, keep moving. MY WHY is the one thing that has carried me through my darkest days! When I was 28 years old, I was told I would never have a baby. It almost destroyed me. I was angry, I was hopeless, I was sad, I was devastated! I will never know how, or why, but 2 years later I gave birth to my miracle baby. I named him Chase because I never stopped chasing the dream of having a baby. The day I gave birth to him, I knew he would be MY WHY, forever! I strive every day to make the world better for him. While I may not actually change the entire world, I work hard to change his world and protect him from the life of generational disasters for which he was destined. There will be hurdles and there will be losses. Just keep moving forward every single day. If you get stuck, get unstuck. If you need help, ask for help early. Do not allow things to fester, that is how it gets out of control. Stay in control of your mindset and keep FEAR in check. Remember, confidence is key. Stay focused on your WHY. The world is your oyster so go find your pearl.

Made in the USA
Columbia, SC
25 September 2024

42359674R00070